Jesus Saves
Yeshua Saves

Testimony of a Former Mason,
Should a Christian Be a Mason?

Dear Godfrey,
thank you for your love and prayers

Jean B Medois
12-1-13

Mr. Jean Bony Medois

ISBN: 061585186X
ISBN-13: 9780615851860

This book is the testimony of a former Mason, one who was deceived, then saved by the power of Jesus. Great insights of the Masonic lodge are given with biblical perspectives.

Yeshua Hamashiach is his name in Hebrew

All scriptures are from the King James Version of the Bible

Jean Bony Medois

Acknowledgements: I give honor and praise to God through Jesus Christ (Yeshua Hamashiach) who has redeemed, saved and provided me with a new life today. It's all about you Lord! If it had not been the Lord who was on my side, I wouldn't be here today.

Thank you to my dad, Letroy Medois, for your love, support, and the gospel which you taught me at an early age. Your life, testimony, faith, and patience in the Lord have impacted me. I thank God for the strength he has given you, as you are still going strong at the age of eighty-two. The Lord has kept you through it all.

To my brothers and family members in Haiti, Europe, and everywhere, a special thank you for your support and prayers.

To Pastor James E. Moore Sr., I thank God for you and your great teachings. You embraced me even when I was not a member of your church. Thank you for pouring out the word in me.

To Archbishop Roy E. Brown of the Pilgrim Assemblies International of Brooklyn, New York. My relationship, knowledge, and faith in the Lord grew rapidly under your leadership in five years. I thank God for using you on many occasions to speak to me from the pulpit about leaving Freemasonry. Thank God for your life!

To Pastor DéBora A. Crowe, thank you for your warm welcome and love during my time at Pilgrim Church.

To Bishop Allen Rivers, you have personally taught me the Bible, behind the wheel, at your dining table, in your living room, and over the phone for three years, and at a level that amazed me. You have truly made me to become a lover of God's word and a defender of the faith. You have been one of the most powerful blessings the Lord has given me in recent years. Your teachings will stay with me. You have changed my life. You have taught me meaningful biblical principles and doctrines. Thank you very much!

To Pastor Edwin Aymat, of the First Baptist Church of Irvington, New Jersey: My first pastor in the United States, thank you for your love toward me and my family during seven great years under your leadership.

To Pastor Mireille Desrosiers and etipm.com (End-Time Intercessory Prayer Ministry, a prayer line), thank you very much for inviting me to teach in your program.

To the members of the Male Choir of my local congregation, thank you for embracing me with love in your midst.

To the members of the Christian Writers Ministry (CWM) of my local congregation, thank you for your support, love and prayers.

Thank you to all the members of Second Baptist Church of Roselle, New Jersey, for your love and support, you have blessed me with since I became a member.

I thank God for all who have contributed to my life. The Lord has blessed me from my childhood with great examples of life and dignity. To my former teachers in Haiti who looked after me, who went beyond teaching to reach out to me in many ways, I dedicate this book to you all and pray that you will have a personal relationship with Jesus Christ.

Finally, a special thanks to all who have prayed for me as well over the years. Your prayers on my behalf have surely been heard and answered.

Thank you,

Brother Jean B. Medois

Table of Contents

A Prayer for All the Readers

Introduction

A Prayer for the Body of Christ Worldwide

A Prayer for All the Readers

Dear Heavenly Father in the mighty name of Jesus Christ (Yeshua Hamashiach), I come before you, covered with your righteousness, by the power of his shed blood that saves and redeems. I thank you! You are great, powerful, and omnipotent.

I bring forth before you today, the readers of this book, which you have inspired me to write for your glory. First, I ask you, Lord, that you forgive us for all of our sins, iniquities, and transgressions. Wash us inside and out with the precious blood of Jesus Christ.

Secondly, Lord, lead all the readers through your Holy Spirit as you reveal to us your written word and the plans of the enemy to deceive us. Allow each of us to have a clear mind to understand the message you have for us.

Thirdly, Lord, I ask you to expose the works of the enemy that would deceive your people. You, Lord, warned us about the counterfeit faiths and doctrines of devils of the last days. Open our spiritual eyes through the light of your written word.

Lord, I pray that you use this book to deliver those in Freemasonry and also in other secret societies which you have not established. Lord, thank you for using me for your glory. Now the time has come for your Holy Spirit to take over.

Save your people, O Lord. Allow us to arrive at the knowledge of your word so that the deceptions of this world will have no power over us. Shield us in your word. Strengthen those that already have a solid relationship with you; establish them even deeper in you.

Bless your people, Lord, to study your word diligently and to preach the gospel to all nations.

Have your way in our lives. May your word set many free today in the name of Jesus (Yeshua), I pray, amen.

Introduction

The purpose of this book is to lift up the name of Jesus (Yeshua) and to appeal to those who are deceived by false teachings and doctrines of this world. I am just allowing God to use me as his instrument to reach out to many that are bound by deceptions of all sorts in this world of darkness.

Before I start with my life story and testimony, let's establish the fact that Jesus is God. Many believe that Christians are polytheists. Not so; we serve only one God who manifests himself in only three ways. *"For there are three that bear record in heaven, the Father, the Word and the Holy Ghost: and these three are one."* (1 John 5:7). If I want to lift up his name and share with you the great things he has done in my life, it is essential that you know who he is. Indeed, who is Jesus Christ (Yeshua Hamashiach)?

Let's think about it for a moment! Let's consider, for example, a man; just pick any name. A husband - that same man could be also a father, a brother, a nephew, a son, a grandson, a business owner, and so on to others. Would you agree? Is that man divided into many parts? No, but that same man is able to play those different roles in his life.

The same applies to God. According to the Bible, God manifests himself only three ways: as the Father, the Son (the Word) and the Holy Spirit and they are one. Many in the world today accuse Christians of serving three gods or idols, but that is just not true.

Now, let's move a little further in establishing the deity of Jesus. There is no better book than the Gospel of John to do that. *"In the beginning was the Word, and the Word was with God, and the Word was God"* (John 1:1). If we connect this verse with 1 John 5:7, we'll clearly understand the term "Word" is referring to Jesus (Yeshua).

Let's go further. Do you remember the prophet Isaiah some four hundred years prior to the birth of Jesus, who prophesied that the Messiah would come? Here's what he said: *"For unto us a child is born (Jesus) unto us a Son is given (Jesus): and the government shall be upon his shoulder: and his name shall be called Wonderful (Jesus), Counselor (Jesus), The mighty God (Jesus), The everlasting Father (Jesus), The Prince of Peace (Jesus)"* (Isaiah 9:6).

Amazingly, the puzzle is coming together, right? So, Jesus is all that? The mighty God, the everlasting Father? It's getting interesting!

So, if Jesus is the everlasting Father, let us go back to the Gospel of John 1:14 *"And the Word (see 1 John 5:7) was made flesh and dwell among us…"* Now, if we look at this verse here in the light of Isaiah 9:6, the mighty God or the everlasting Father, came down in the flesh to dwell among us. The apostle Paul confirmed this: *"And without controversy great is the mystery of godliness: God was manifest in the flesh, justified in the Spirit, seen of angels, preached unto the Gentiles, believed on in the world, received up into glory."* (1 Timothy 3:16).

We are not done yet! Let's look here at what Jesus said, when he dwelt among us: *"I and my Father are one"* (John 10:30). Now, here is what the angel of the Lord said to Joseph about the birth of Jesus: *"Behold, a virgin shall be with child, and shall bring forth a son, and they shall call his name Imman'u-el, which being interpreted is, God with us."* (Matthew 1:23).

"I am Alpha and Ome'ga, the beginning and the ending, saith the Lord, which is, and was, and which is to come, the Almighty." (Revelation 1:8). Now, if I ask anyone, "Who is the Alpha and Omega?" and "Who is the beginning and the ending?" I am sure that the answer would be God or Jehovah, right? Now, let's go a bit further to Revelation 22:13: *"I am Alpha and Ome'ga, the beginning and the end, the first and the last."* Once again, the answer would be unanimous: That's God, right?

Let's see how God of the Old Testament is identified with in the New Testament. Please follow me to the Old Testament book of Isaiah, *"Thus saith the LORD THE KING OF ISRAEL, AND HIS REDEEMER THE LORD OF HOSTS; I am the first, and I am the last; and beside me there is no God."* (Isaiah 44:6).

Let's go back to the New Testament book of Revelation 1:17-18: *"And when I saw him, I fell at his feet as dead. And he laid his right hand upon me, saying unto me, Fear not: <u>I am the first and the last: I am he that liveth, and was dead; and behold, I am alive for evermore.</u>* Amen; and have the keys of hell and of death."* To back it up, let's go to Revelation 2:8, *"And unto the angel of the church in Smyrna write; these things saith <u>the first and the last,</u> which <u>was dead, and is alive."</u>*

Now, <u>when did God or Jehovah die? Who died and rose again?</u> That settles it! Clearly, we see how the eternal God of the Old Testament revealed himself or is identified as Jesus (Yeshua) in the New Testament. Indeed, I rest my case: <u>Jesus (Yeshua) is God!</u>

Since, we have established that Jesus is God and God manifests himself only three ways - as, the Father, the Son, and the Holy Spirit, what about all of the other ways or religions that have been out there through the centuries? Doesn't the Bible address that? God forewarned us about the tactical play of the devil to duplicate and create other false ways to deceive mankind. *"Jesus saith unto him, I am the way, the truth, and the life: no man cometh unto the Father, but by me."* (John 14:6). A prophetic aspect is attached to this verse. We can connect it with the prophecies of Jesus in Matthew 24, when he talked to his disciples about the deceptions of the last days. There are many other ways duplicated falsely by the devil, but only one way to eternal salvation: Jesus Christ.

Many think that Christians are arrogant because we claim he (Jesus) is the only way, but that's what the Bible says. We do not have to rely on people's opinions, since the Bible is the revealed and spoken word of God. It is not about what you and I think, or what society wants us to believe, but rather what is written in his word.

Jesus Christ is the one that I will be talking about throughout this book. I'll tell you my life story, my testimonies, and how he saved me from one of the most deceptive tools used by the enemy to deceive humanity and to infiltrate the body of Christ.

Chapter 1

A Painful Childhood

I was born on March 25, 1975, in Haiti. My mom and dad served the Lord and therefore provided Christian values to all of us. I am the third child of five, and we all grew up together at 71 Rue Joseph Janvier in the capital city. As I write these lines, I feel very emotional about my childhood, which was marked by illnesses, hospitalizations, and frequent visits to clinics and medical labs. I thank God for a praying dad, Letroy Medois, who is still living at the age of eighty-two. The Lord raised him up in the 1970s to preach the gospel, and he also became the leader of a prayer ministry that held services every noon at our house. In our neighborhood, which was located about four or five blocks from the presidential palace, our home was known for its constant noise as we hosted multiple prayer services.

When I was about two years old, my life took a sad turn that shaped me to this day. Illnesses, sicknesses, humiliations, fears, anxiety, pains became the characteristics of my young life. It appeared that none of them were normal, for I was vaccinated properly like my brothers. Here, were some of my burdens:

- Typhoid fever

- Tuberculosis

- constipation

- constant and frequent vomiting

- severe arthritis and stiffness

- eye problems

- bad skin condition with open wounds all over my body

- constant sore throat

- lung infections

- speech impairment

These were among the symptoms that kept me away from a normal childhood for years. Witchcraft attacks bombarded me. Doctors couldn't get to the bottom of my maladies. I watched from bed, all of my brothers growing up healthy. I looked horrible; I was very skinny with infections on top of all kinds of physical and medical problems that went on for some eight years.

It's like a dream to me to think about the way my immune system was so weak that I had a constant, annoying, and loud cough. Parents sometimes, asked my teachers not to allow me to sit near their children. At some point in my childhood, I could see my mother giving up on me (her faith was pretty weak) but my dad always kept his faith up high and, strong. He believed that one day, I would be healed. I thank God for my father's faith that never faltered at the distractions that came his ways. One of my uncles even told him to stop spending money on me.

It seemed like, I was way too young to endure all that but God was on my side throughout the whole ordeal because he created me for his own purpose.

I remember some of the conversations between my parents about how worried they were that the school would send me back home, just for the other children's sakes, regarding, health concerns. But it never happened because during a couple of years when things got really bad for me, I stayed home or in hospitals because of my conditions. Even when I sometimes missed two to three months of schooling, the Lord still allowed me to be among the best students at the end of the school year.

Let me share with you a testimony from my dad that took place in 1977. I was about two years old when I suddenly became sick. My parents rushed me to the hospital by catching a cab. It was the quickest way for them to reach the hospital. At their arrival, they met a famous doctor by the name of Bartoli. He was known at that time for his accurate death predictions. He made a name for himself in Haiti just because of that.

According to my dad, I was diagnosed with typhoid, constipation, fluids in my lungs and the list goes on and on. Dr. Bartoli examined me (a little baby) and declared to my parents that I was so sick, if I didn't get operated on by four o'clock that afternoon, I would die. It turned out on that day, I was not operated on. The doctor himself passed away a couple of months later.

Although, it was not easy for me to grow up like that, eight years of my childhood were spent between my sick-bed, hospitals, clinics, and labs. I swallowed tons of pills and medications. My stomach was always messed up to the point that nothing could stay in. Throwing up was frequent in my life, and I even vomited water. That situation did not go well with my mom. She used to wake up early to prepare healthy and nutritious breakfasts for me, just to see it on the floor right after.

I remember being hospitalized at St. François de Salle in 1984. My lungs were in a bad condition, and the doctors had to set a breathing machine right on my face that sprayed out medicated air to help me breathe. In fact, I also had tuberculosis.

I became bitter and hateful especially towards the doctors and nurses that constantly applied needle sticks to my arms for medications to get in. At some point the pains were unbearable. I was always in tears, trying to figure out why I couldn't play, eat, or be healthy like my brothers and most children in general.

I grew up with a huge deficiency in terms of nutrition, which is still visible on my body up to this day, because of constant vomiting. At the time my body needed those nutrients to develop, it did not receive them. Up to this day, my hands, arms, and legs are so thin that they are the sizes of those belonging to a normal nine or a ten-year-old. My legs are so skinny that I've never in my life, up to this day, put on short pants to go out. You see, things that some take for granted could be a big deal for others. Only my brothers and parents know about the appearance of my legs, along with the years of scares that just added to the ordeal. God leaves those signs on me for a purpose, as a reminder of where he took me from, and to keep me humble.

Even now, when I shake someone's hands, it is noticeable how bony mine are. God allowed me to go through it all because he was and he is still with me. He chastens whom he loves. Once again, I thank him for the unshakable faith of my dad, whom the devil tried to lead in different directions. The devil sent his disciples one after another to deter his faith, but he always believed that God would heal me. One day, one of his prayer partners, a ministry leader like him, came to him and declared: "that illness is a shame." He had never seen anything like it - a child being sick for that long, when even prayers and doctors couldn't get to the bottom of it. Let me tell you now, that God turned those ashes to something he can use today. He's still in the business of healing and restoring, no matter how it looks today.

For more than eight years, I suffered like no one could ever imagine in a lifetime. The humiliations I went through from those at school and the neighborhood, and those that relentlessly mocked me because of my physical appearance, had a toll on me. The way I walked as a child, caused many to make fun of me, because of the arthritis pains and stiffness my body went through for years. I walk like an old man, some have said, even to this day. On the top of it all, I have suffered from a speech disorder, which I would call the most advanced form of stuttering. In fact, I was not supposed to be able to speak at all. It would take me a long time just to get one word out, with a lot of grimacing as well. A little bit of stuttering is still around from time to time but not the way it used to be in my childhood.

I have nothing against those parents that didn't want their children around me, with the infections on my skins and my constant cough. The risk of being contaminated was understandable. I looked like a monster; I was extremely skinny, with bad skin and scales like a fish all over my body. At some point in the 1980s, my body became very stiff, which I carry with me up until today. It was very painful to walk, or even to take one step every time I woke up.

Nevertheless, things got darker. My health deteriorated during 1985 and that I had to be hospitalized. I remember telling my mom about my dreams during the nights because she always asked me about them. I used to see people in those dreams that wanted to take my life away but on the other hand someone always stood up on my side to stop the way of the wicked. Doctors gave up on me during that year, and my mom literally did so. In one of the darkest nights of my life, I found myself in a dark room on a terrible Friday night. It was supposed to be my last day, as I was expected to die. My parents emptied a bedroom that usually contained three beds of my brothers and left me in that room to die away from them.

My dad spent most of the night, at my bed-side, praying for me, while my mom got up a couple of times during the night to see if I was still alive. I remember clearly seeing her shadow at the room's entrance, sticking her neck forward to take a look at me. My dad asked me to confess Jesus Christ, and I did.

The Lord, my Savior Jesus Christ, was on my side; he carried me through the darkest moment of my life. During that same year, the Lord healed me from that long and painful ordeal, from that long period of sickness and shame. The Lord rolled it away because of the fervent prayer of my dad and many others. Although the Lord allows the marks of that burden to remain on me, he healed me completely and has allowed me to enjoy relatively good health since 1985.

Even though, I was healed, I grew up with a rebellious spirit towards the things of God. We have had prayers daily at home, but I played all kinds of games to stay away from prayer services. Once in a while, my dad would whip me for not being grateful to God and the healing he provided for me. Nevertheless, he prophesied on me multiple times, on how the Lord would use me, but I always rebuked it all with anger towards him and God. I didn't want to serve the Lord at all; the darkness of the world and its influences were catching up on me. My parents were very strict and wouldn't allow us to even stand on the sidewalk or go to the carnival which took place only a few blocks away.

Thank God for a praying and faithful dad. Even with our rebellious nature, he taught us the Bible and forced us to pray. I grew up not serving the Lord at all. After high school, I had more freedom to leave the house, and I found myself in a position where I had multiple women whom I was involved with.

My mom left Haiti to migrate to the United States in 1987. Dad was left behind to take care of us. The socio-economic situation of the country deteriorated and we couldn't wait to leave Haiti. Eventually, after twelve long years of waiting, we made it here in the United States. We landed at JFK Airport on Sunday, July 4, 1999. It was amazing to me, coming from the poorest country in the western hemisphere to the most powerful one. However, my spiritual life hadn't changed at all. In fact, I went deeper into living a sinful life.

I attended church out of tradition, but I was very rebellious against my God who had saved me from a sick childhood. However, I attended college and did pretty well by graduating with a bachelor's degree in accounting. There, the devil brought up a stronghold on me that only God had the ability to deliver me from. My sinful life became unbearable to the point that I completely gave up on any idea of deliverance and I knew the end result was death. I couldn't help it. The fact is that America is such a rich country; it offered me even more opportunities to sin. I started to travel to Las Vegas to party. Night and strip clubs became my way of life, until the Lord made a move in 2006 to reclaim me.

Chapter 2

My Initiation into Freemasonry

The Biggest Mistake of My Life, but the Lord Has Turned it for His Glory

The events that led to my conversion to Jesus Christ (Yeshua Hamashiach) were quite remarkable. I was living a sinful life that kept me away from church for most of 2006. Parties, sex, and watching television became the norm. I opened the door to demonic manifestations in my life unknowingly. Truly, I departed from the Lord but the bible is true as it is written: *"Train up a child in the way he should go: and when he is old, he will not depart from it."* (Proverbs 22:6). My parents did their part but it was then for the Lord to do his.

In that same year, the Lord was about to claim what was already his, but the devil made a great move in order to stop it from happening. I became addicted to football and I wouldn't go to church. When the congregants asked me, "Where have you been?" I always found an excuse or a lie to tell. Then, I started to have unusual dreams where demons and wicked men came to threaten me and even kill me. I didn't quite know what to do, except to turn to a good friend of mine for spiritual advice.

The devil is more deceitful than you can imagine. It turned out that I inquired about help to the wrong individual. My friend advised me to join Freemasonry as a way to find the light and deliverance. There is tremendous power in it, according to him. I was initiated as an Entered Apprentice in the Masonic community in the midst of tremendous demonic attacks, on November 18, 2006. I barely slept that whole week for fear of having those dreams; I was extremely tired and weak. I couldn't truly concentrate on the ceremony. On that day, I received a Masonic Bible and a white apron, which symbolizes purity. It is asked of every Mason to keep it until death, that you may be buried with it if you desire. Later on, I realized that their beliefs and philosophy are such that, if you play by the rules and follow Masonic principles, be good to society, and be charitable, your soul as a Mason will be ordered into the heavenly lodge. This is totally different from what the Bible teaches (for Jesus is the only way) but I didn't know any better.

There were thirty-eight men on that day, from seven Masonic temples, within the same district, who were initiated. The initiation lasted the whole day. When it was all over, I quickly said Good-bye to everyone and jumped into my car and headed home just to sleep. I slept like a baby that afternoon, like I hadn't slept in months.

My life then turned south. That same night, the demonic attacks intensified. I spent that whole night with my lights and TV on, just refusing to sleep because of those dreams. The next day was Sunday, I didn't go to church. I was comforted by the daylight and went to bed around nine in the morning. I got up around eleven to find myself in a forceful fight. My apartment shook sporadically; I heard weird noises and a hand that kept pounding at the walls. I started to pray and call upon the Lord, but it seemed like the more I prayed the worse it became. Then, at noon sharp, the Mason who had encouraged me to join, called me. It was like he knew exactly what was going on because of the questions he asked me. He came right away, since he lived only a few minutes away.

According to what I explained to him, he suggested that I come with him and spend the night over at his place. I knew he was also a Christian, but as I spent time there, I saw strange things in his apartment. At the bottoms of the doors, there were plates of sea salt topped by candles lying down. I didn't ask him any questions as I saw more strange and mystical items. Before we went to sleep, he invited me to pray with him. He stood up, facing the east, and asked me to do the same. He placed three lit candles in a pyramidal position on the floor, right in front of us. Something was going on but I couldn't tell what it was. The truth of the matter was that he wanted to take me to a deeper level of Satanism. He explained to me how he could help me become invisible to others and even find out who was persecuting me. I never really paid attention to him because I was naive, and also because of the fact that I needed him to teach me the Bible, he had spent four years in Bible school.

The trend of events continued and on November 21, 2006, I was admitted to Trinitas Hospital in Elizabeth, New Jersey. There, in a short-term mental facility, the biggest event of my life was about to unfold.

Chapter 3

My Conversion to Jesus Christ

(Yeshua Hamashiach)

Three days after my initiation into Freemasonry, the Lord showed up powerfully in my life with his outstretched and mighty hands. I found myself in a short-term mental facility in Elizabeth, New Jersey, at Trinitas Hospital. There, the Lord Jesus (Yeshua) came and met me. The following took place from November 21 to November 27 of the year 2006.

One morning after breakfast, I sat down in the TV room where the patients had gathered to watch some morning shows. There was a young lady whom I had not seen for a day or so. She suffered from depression and was under heavy medications; she'd stay a whole day in her room to sleep because of the side effects of those medicines. That particular morning, she was different. She was very alert as she came and sat in our midst. Patricia was her first name. She was a regular patient at the facility and everyone knew her. Something amazed me and caught my attention quickly: Every time I saw her around, she carried a Bible. Although she was depressed, that Bible was always with her.

On that morning, she came in the room and had a conversation with some of the other patients. Suddenly, she got up and came straight to me. She stood up in front of me while engaging me in a conversation. We both introduced ourselves to each other. Quickly, she asked if she could sit next to me because she had something to tell me. I said, "OK."

As Patricia started to talk to me, her face changed and became a bit reddish. She mentioned to me how the Lord had used her in the past to bring forth his word to many, and that God was using her right now to speak directly to me. She told me that I was chosen to bring forth the gospel to the nations and that I would become a preacher.

I was stunned and angry because I hated the idea of being a preacher, even deep inside my soul. Patricia's face turned totally red and her voice became louder and louder as everyone else in the room diverted their attention toward us. All of the patients in the room heard the sermon that lasted for about twenty to twenty-five minutes. During the conversation, I realized that she had prophesied the exact thing that I heard from my dad, even during my lamented childhood. She said to me, "Jean, there's nothing wrong with you. God brought you up here for a reason. You're not sick, but I am."

I knew deep inside that, she was telling the truth, but on the other hand, a part of me was rebuking it. I kept saying to myself, "My dream is to become an accountant, get my own practice down the road, and make a lot of money."

At the end, Patricia asked me if she could possibly lay hands and pray for me. I must also mention that she is Hispanic. She said to me, "I'll pray in Spanish. I feel more comfortable like that; will that be OK with you? "

"No problem." I told her. Even though, I know Spanish a bit, I couldn't understand what she was praying about as she laid both hands on me. I heard a bunch of "Padre Dios, Señor, gracias, etc..." As she ended her prayer, she said to me "Remember my face; I'll see you in the future preaching the gospel."

After she had left, I entered into a deep reflection. A battle started in my mind about what she had told me versus my own desires and aspirations. After thorough analysis and thoughts, I decided to rebuke and to clear my mind from everything she had ministered to me. I even convinced myself that the reason she had come to me was that she needed a man. After all that, I went back to square one! Now, as I am writing this piece, I can understand how the devil operates in our minds. This is his primary battleground. Nevertheless, God is faithful!

One or two days after that encounter, I sat down in the same TV room. It was in the afternoon this time around, a little while after lunch. Most patients were either in their rooms or in the hallways. My eyes were focused on the TV screen, watching an early afternoon show. Suddenly, I noticed a big man sitting across the room about two or three yards away from me. His eyes were on me, I mean staring at me continually. I was bothered by the fact that he was a total stranger to me, but he kept on looking at me constantly. At some point, I left the room just to take a walk away from him, just to see his reactions and what his intentions were, and then I came right back. He was a huge, heavy-set type of man, Hispanic, and dressed like a cowboy. He wore boots, and his face was unfamiliar to me. I got to know the patients on my floor very well because we ate together four times a day, had activities together, and so forth. There was no doubt in my mind that I had not seen him before.

After a while, he got up and came straight to me. "I have something to tell you." he exclaimed. "I've been looking at you for a while; have you noticed?"

I said, "Yes."

"When you got up and left the room to take a walk, I got up as well; I looked at you walking down the hallway with someone next to you. You came back and sat down, and he sat next to you. Everywhere you go, he's with you. Why don't you put your trust in him?" he said to me.

I was speechless as he started to raise his voice, "Why don't you put your trust in him?" he kept saying, literally yelling at me. Then, he started to preach the gospel to me, still with a loud voice. That time around, God sent someone to exhort me even in a more powerful way, for he was not willing to let me go. The more the man talked to me, the more excited he became.

The time came for dinner, and we went together. Along the way, the man never stopped preaching the gospel to me. He reiterated most of what Patricia had told me about myself. Unfortunately, I couldn't understand back then what confirmation from the Lord means. I was so surprised that I kept my mouth shut the whole time, listening to the man. When I reflect now about it, I can see how great God is. The messenger that time around had a dominant presence and a loud voice.

His size was of a defensive lineman in football; he was a dominant figure and therefore I had to yield and listen to him.

God knew what he was doing. When I didn't want to listen to a sweet woman's voice, he sent an imposing figure to dominate my rebellious countenance. The man, or messenger, kept preaching the gospel to me. In the dining room, he got up and knocked on the table many times and said, "Why don't you put your trust in him?" over and over again, to the point of getting the attention of the others in the room. After dinner, we stayed a little while in the dining room alone while I continued to listen carefully to him ministering to me. About thirty minutes later, we walked back to the TV room and I sat down next to him again. He had never stopped talking and preaching to me. I mean, he was a real talking machine.

After a while, I started to make it a dialogue as I had thought about giving up my life to Christ. I wasn't fully convinced because I had always thought about ways to get away from God. He introduced himself to me and I did the same. He noticed my accent and asked me where I was from.

"Haiti." I said.

Then, the messenger said to me, "I belong to an all-Haitian church in Irvington, New Jersey. I am the only Hispanic in that church. I like to worship with the Haitian people." Surprisingly, he mentioned a few French and Creole words to me as I told him that his pronunciation wasn't bad at all.

As the hours went by, we continued with our conversation. I couldn't hold myself anymore. I had to surrender my life to Jesus. I couldn't run away from his calling anymore.

The messenger told me that he had just been admitted to the hospital. "I don't know what's wrong with me, or why I am here. Perhaps, the Lord sent me here only for you."

My whole attitude towards God had changed at that time. "Please excuse me; let me get my Bible in my room. I'll be right back!" I said to him. In fact, I had no idea how the Bible had come with me to the hospital. I came back and sat next to him again.

The Bible in my hands, I prayed to God and gave my life to him, I surrendered. I didn't want to run away from his presence anymore. I gave up my life to Jesus Christ that night while God's messenger was sitting next to me witnessing the event. It was the time for me to bring all my burdens to him, the true and living God. I prayed another prayer and asked the Lord, as I was about to start reading the word, to guide me to wherever he wanted me to read. Quickly, I opened up my Bible and went straight to the book of Job. I knew deep on the inside that God himself directed me to that book for a reason which I did not know at that time. I had such a great appetite and desire to read God's word like never before. I read the first twenty chapters of that book. Snack was served around nine or so, and I have never seen the man since then.

The next day, I was discharged from the hospital. The psychiatrist prescribed--Risperdal--to me, to be taken once a day at nine before bedtime. Then, my biggest fear was that: I did not have health insurance. I knew that the hospital bill would be coming soon. About a year or so, prior to my hospitalization, I was denied New Jersey charity care; they stated that my income as a substitute teacher was too high considering the fact that I was single also. I made a bit more than I had at that time, and I thought that there was no way; I would qualify this time around. Nevertheless, the hospital administration suggested that I apply again for charity care, and perhaps they would pick up a portion or a small percentage of the bill. I did so doubtfully, and waited for about two or three weeks. One day, I received a letter in the mail. The hospital bill was around eighteen thousand dollars for six days of hospitalization. The bill was fully paid. Thank you, Jesus! God showed up early in my new life. *"O give thanks unto the Lord; for he is good: because his mercy endureth for ever."* (Psalm 118:1).

Right after that, a tremendous test was waiting for me. My mother's condition headed for the worse, to the point that doctors asked her to stop working. She was diagnosed with a terminal illness called dermatomyositis. According to the doctors, there was no hope, although they had tried their best. I had to empty out my apartment and, threw all my belongings in the garbage, because she needed someone to take care of her on a daily basis. So, I went back to live with her to facilitate, for my dad doesn't drive neither speak English. Five to six doctors were on the case. We had multiple doctors' visits as I drove her around from time to time. She became weaker and weaker, to the point that I had to stop working to concentrate more on her. I became overwhelmed by her malady. It was one of the biggest challenges I've ever faced in my life. I started to pray to God and asked him for strength and to heal my mom, but her situation deteriorated. In March of 2007, she had to be hospitalized, and later on she was transferred to intensive care.

I'll never forget that moment when around one o'clock in the morning, I received a call from the hospital. It was frightening as the doctor told me, "Her lungs collapsed." My brothers had come from different states to say good-bye to her, and I let them know about the call I had received. We managed to get to the hospital. Around two in the morning, they allowed us to see her. She was hooked up to a machine that was literally breathing for her. At that time, I had no income coming in. For some reasons, many people including family members came to visit my unconscious mom and left either one hundred or two hundred dollars for me. This did not happen once or twice, but many times. I used those funds to pay for my regular bills. God is my way-maker!

While my mother was in intensive care, I spent my days at the hospital at her side and I also visited funeral homes, preparing for the inevitable, but the Lord touched her. She got stronger and stronger, to the point of being discharged about twenty days later. After four months, she went back to work and that was a surprise to all of us. Our church (the First Baptist Church of Irvington, New Jersey) came to our home and brought a celebration of praise for that miracle. The Lord was molding, shaping and even purging me through the entire ordeal.

Although, two years later, I lost my mom, (she was sixty-two) I still thank God for her life. I was blessed enough to have the love and guidance of a mother for thirty four years of my life.

As God is the potter and we are the clay, we can become in his hands, through the tests, trials and tribulations all that he created us to be, and it shall come to pass in the mighty name of Jesus (Yeshua).

Chapter 4

A Terrible Car Accident

What the Devil Meant for Evil, God Used It According to His Will and Purpose for My Life

"I shall not die, but live, and declare the works of the Lord."

Psalm 118:17

What I am about to explain might sound surreal, but it's the truth. I thank my Lord and Savior Jesus Christ (Yeshua Hamashiach) for saving me and giving me a tangible proof (the police report) to back up my testimony. One of the definitions of the word "miracle" that I like the most goes like this: *an extraordinary event manifesting divine intervention in human affairs.*

Sometimes, the human mind cannot understand the works of God. Three months after the family buried mom, I found myself in a deep spiritual and financial pit. I was more than a month behind in rent, three collection agencies were calling constantly, bills were piling up, and I was depressed. It was one of those moments when I felt that God was totally absent from my life.

On November 19, 2009, I had to pick my dad up from the Newark Airport. He had come from California, where my mom spent the rest of her life. He came back to New Jersey to attend the funeral of a close friend to the family. For some reasons, I kept hearing the words "car accident" in my ears sporadically. I managed to run away from that thought every time. Nevertheless, all went well on that day; it was good to see dad in great shape only months after he had lost his wife.

On the next day, November the twentieth, all was about to change for me, I'd never be the same again. It was a beautiful morning. As the sun rose in the bright blue sky, I got behind the wheel to go to work. Then, around seven thirty, I managed to make a slight left turn. My eyes got caught up in the sunshine, and that hit my eyes and blinded me for one or two seconds. The size of the risen sun at that time of the year is bigger than usual. It was so huge, right above the earth's surface. It hit my eyes so hard, and my car collided head-on, with bus 21 near downtown Newark on West Market Street.

"Thy testimonies are wonderful; therefore doth my soul keep them."

Psalm 119:125

Immediately, I couldn't feel myself. I was numb, and strangely I thought I was dead. Quickly, I realized I was not, as I looked left and right to notice that my lips were moving constantly. That's when I knew I was alive. I kept repeating in French "Jésus, Jésus, Jésus". Now, I was convinced I was alive, and I saw the front of the bus right in front of my car.

I jumped out of my car (a 2008 Mazda6) and knocked at the bus door. The bus driver kept the door closed; I guess that was proper procedure before the police and other authorities arrived at the scene. Then, I moved to the driver's side to talk to him. I could see the anger on his face as he told me, "You make me sick." After that, my mind started to grasp the magnitude of the accident. I got closer to my car and saw the front destroyed completely. The car was dead on the spot, and a bit of smoke was coming out. I grabbed my phone and called my job to let them know I couldn't make it because of what had just taken place.

"Thy testimonies also are my delight and my counselors."

Psalm 119:24

About ten minutes later, the police and a Newark fire truck arrived at the scene. They found me standing next to my car, my cell phone in my hand, talking to the secretary at my job. My mind was empty and I tried to figure out what had just happened. Was I dreaming or not? Could this really happen to me? I asked myself. I remember, seeing a woman driving with her child in the back-seat, pointing at the scene, bursting out laughing with a sense of mocking the event. That's when I realized the devil had just showed himself to me. I'm not saying she's the devil, but she was just being used, just like God uses his children. *"Thou hast thrust sore at me that I might fall: but the Lord helped me."* (Psalm 118:13). As the minutes went by, I realized how great of a miracle the Lord Jesus had done for me.

I believe the firefighters were the first to investigate the accident; they asked a couple of questions. They also tested the condition of the ground. Then, the police investigation began. One officer took me back to the car. He opened the door of the vehicle, to look on the inside, and I noticed that none of the airbags had come out. I had bought the car in 2008, brand new, and about a year and a half later the airbags had failed to deploy. The car had front and side airbags, and with that kind of impact, it was unbelievable that they would not have deployed! By the way, it was rush hour; the bus probably had thirty to forty passengers on it.

Thank God, that all of the passengers did not need medical care. I couldn't believe it! I had gotten out of that car, with that kind of impact, healthy and whole. *"O give thanks unto the Lord for he is good: because his mercy endureth forever."* (Psalm 118:1). The impact had no effects on me when the vehicles (David and Goliath) collided. I did not feel the shock at all; believe me, I'm not lying. I felt like a cushion took the burden for me. I sat straight behind the wheel and no parts of my body were hurt. In fact, I came out of the car with no injuries, not even a slight headache. The works of the Lord were just wonders in my life that morning.

The name of the Lord is my high tower and my refuge. <u>When my eyes and the airbags failed me, Jesus (Yeshua) did not.</u> It was quite amazing to the officers, especially the one that lead the investigation, to see me standing and, in my right mind, and answering all the questions they threw at me. Suddenly, I saw two paramedics escorting the bus driver to the ambulance. From what I heard at the scene, his blood pressure went so high that they had to rush him to the hospital. His back bent forward while being helped to leave the bus. Nevertheless, I refused medical care. I felt the same way I had at the time I got in the car that morning. The investigation continued as New Jersey Transit, the bus company, sent an investigator at the scene. He started by taking pictures of the vehicles at different angles.

Then - it was his turn to question me. We talked for about five minutes. He even told me he had come to investigate a couple of accidents prior to mine at that same spot. The location is known to have similar accidents because of much-needed traffic lights. Not to make any excuses--but without a test, there is no testimony. The Bible says, *"And we know that all things work together for good to them that love God, to them who are the called according to his purpose."* (Romans 8:28). So it is true; if it had not been for that accident, my faith wouldn't be where it is today. Sometimes, we don't know why we go through so much in life, but let me tell you that God has a purpose for it all. We are his workmanship. He said, *"For my thoughts are not your thoughts, neither are your ways my ways, saith the Lord. For as the heavens are higher than the earth, so are my ways higher than your ways, and my thoughts than your thoughts."* (Isaiah 55:8-9).

Be assured, the Christian life is not an easy one, but we are not left comfortless or alone. Jesus said to his disciples, in a verse that always come to my mind, from the Gospel of John: *"These things I have spoken unto you that, in me ye might have peace. In the world ye shall have tribulation; but be of good cheer; I have overcome the world."* (John 16:33). What a comforting statement from our Lord! Notice, the English translation uses "shall" which means it is a must. Just like Jesus said to his disciples, if you want to follow me, you have to carry the cross.

I remember, before I came to know the Lord Jesus Christ, money had not been an issue. The more I spent to sin, the more money came to my pocket and bank accounts. Money was at my fingertips for wherever I wanted to go to party, such as in Las Vegas. After my conversion, all that went on the flip side. Money dried out--I mean, there was a severe drought of cash caused by long periods of unemployment and, the inability to find a well-paying job in the field in which I studied, and so on. Sometimes, discouragements and thoughts to give up Christ to the world crossed my mind. The devil is a liar, but God is a way-maker! Sometimes, he won't move or calm the storm, but with his mighty hands, he can take you and carry you through it. We do serve a mighty God!

Back at the accident scene, the police ordered both vehicles to be towed. Although, there was no apparent damage to the front of the bus, they had to follow proper procedure. On the other hand, my car was disabled on the spot. An officer got behind the wheel while others pushed it to the side of the road to relieve traffic in the area. The tow truck came and I did not realize it had been the last time I would ever drive my car. Indeed, a few weeks later, the insurance company declared the car, totaled. No big deal! The devil had me to die that day on his calendar, but Jesus said, "Not so!" Aren't you glad you're not living according to the devil's plan for your life? Even, if the Lord allows a few things to reach us, it is for his purpose, for his glory to be manifested in us. The truth of the matter is that accident brought me to a higher level of faith, trust, and understanding of God.

So, the vehicles were towed, the investigations were over, and the traffic was cleared and back to normal as I walked two blocks up to catch one of the first two buses I needed to get back home. I was pretty sad to walk on my feet and wait for a bus. It was unusual to me. I felt a sense of humiliation. That was the wrong way for me to look at things that morning. I could have been dead, paralyzed, severely injured with broken bones and so on, but none of these happened. I was very well physically on that day. The Lord protected me when I couldn't do it myself. Instead of going home and telling dad, I changed my mind and stopped at the Roselle Park library, which was located about seven minutes from my place. There, I got my thoughts together on how to proceed. I had a very important funeral to attend the next day. I needed a car right away. I went online and reserved a car for the same day at Enterprise Rent-A-Car. I sat at the library for hours and left at about three to pick up the vehicle.

The entire ordeal looks like a supernatural script written and orchestrated by God himself for his purpose. The fact is that the testimony did not stop there but continued throughout that day. At about three thirty in the afternoon (on the same day of course) I went back to driving, just like nothing had taken place that morning. Thank you, Jesus! My mind was cleared from the accident and I drove on the Garden State Parkway, back to Newark and the University of Medicine and Dentistry of New Jersey (UMDNJ) police headquarters to obtain a police release that was needed for the release of my vehicle to a mechanic. Unbelievable!

I do not know why God loves me so much. When I think about the weight of the bus itself plus those thirty or so passengers on it, I am speechless. He spared my life. I have shared my testimony since that time with many people and churches, and I have also shared copies of the police report. The Psalmist said, *"I will speak of thy testimonies also before kings and will not be ashamed."* (Psalm 119:111). In fact, in August 2010 I heard the Holy Spirit say to me, "Copies, copies, copies." at that same Roselle Park library. I understood that I needed to make a ton of them (police report) to share with others about the goodness of the Lord in my life.

This testimony is very precious to me; I carry it in my thoughts all the time. One day, I sat down in a quiet place, just fellowshipping with my Lord Jesus Christ. I placed a copy of the police report on the table right in front of me. I read it thoroughly just to get a better understanding of it, and also to appreciate my God. Then, I prayed and asked the Lord to put this miracle in perspective for me with a similar one in the Bible. Immediately, the Holy Spirit overtook me and brought up to my remembrance, the story of Daniel and the Hebrew boys. I opened up my Bible and searched for the appropriate chapter: Daniel 3! I read it through and the Holy Spirit mentioned the twenty-seventh verses to me. That was all I ever needed. *"And the princes, governors, and captains, and the king's counselors, being gathered together, saw these men, upon whose bodies the fire had no power, nor was a hair of their head singed, neither were their coats changed, nor the smell of fire had passed on them."* (Daniel 3:27).

This is the kind of God we serve. There were no traces of the accident on me. The next day, I drove to the funeral with my father at my side. I hadn't told him about the accident then. I just mentioned to him that my vehicle had a problem and I rented the one I drove. On our trip to the cemetery, one of the deacons of the church, a close friend to my family, rode with us. In our conversation, he said I would become a pastor. I heard that so many times in my life. Perhaps, that was one of the reasons why the devil made a move to kill me before I reached my destiny. If God said it, that settles it. It shall come to pass.

*"I have kept thy precepts and thy testimonies: for all
my ways are before thee."*

Psalm 119:168

Now the Spirit speaketh expressly, that in the latter times some shall depart from the faith, giving heed to seducing spirits, and doctrines of devils.

I Timothy 4:1

Chapter 5

My Calling

One of My First Major Assignments from the Lord

After I resigned from both the Blue Lodge and the Scottish Rite, the Lord quickly turned me around by giving me many opportunities to minister to Masons in the streets, on buses, at my job and also in churches. At some point, it became a daily routine, and the Lord guided me every step of the way. It was amazing to see how God set men on my path that had Masonic signs on themselves and on their cars, as I ministered the word of God to them. As months are passed by, the Lord kept on increasing my responsibility by giving me major assignments.

One day, at the end of November 2010, I met a bishop in a pharmacy as I stood in line to pick up my dad's medications. I went straight to him and introduced myself. We joked and laughed. Cordially, we spoke to each other as he handed me his business card and asked me to come on over to visit his church whenever I could. I took the business card and stored it in my wallet.

On Martin Luther King, Jr. Day of 2011, I dedicated myself to seeking God's face in prayer and fasting. I heard the Holy Spirit asking me to call a certain pastor, to find out about his stands on Freemasonry. I did, and we met later on that day. We spoke for about two hours on Freemasonry and false teachings and worldly influences in the body of Christ. That particular pastor is against Freemasonry, but in our conversation he brought up the name of that bishop, as a well-known Mason, the man I had met a couple of months prior. I knew deep within, that God did not reveal that to me by accident.

A few months later, on a Saturday morning as I was taking a shower, the Holy Spirit fell heavily upon me as I heard, "You are going to write a letter to Bishop So-and-so." As soon as I heard that, the Lord started to provide me with the questions and arguments I needed to ask him in the letter. I had to jump out of the shower, and grabbed a pen and a piece of paper to write them down quickly. I spent a good part of the day at the library to plan the letter carefully. Here is the text:

To: Bishop So-and-so

From: Brother Jean Medois

Re: Freemasonry

Date: xx- 01-11

I greet you, Bishop, in the name of our Lord Jesus Christ (Yeshua Hamashiach). My name is Jean Medois, a follower of Jesus living in the area. A few months ago, I met you at the CVS pharmacy. We spoke for a few minutes, and you gave me your business card. I don't think it was a coincidence, for God does all things for a reason.

A year ago, Bishop, the Lord delivered me from one of the schemes that the devil is using to deceive mankind. I'm a former Thirty-Second degree in the Scottish Rite and former member of a Blue Lodge. I served as a Junior Steward and a Marshal. I was named to become a chaplain when the Lord intervened and caused me to quit. It took me two years from ignoring repeated calls from God through my bishop to leave Freemasonry. It is clear that sometimes in his messages he will go off to expose Freemasonry, and the Lord did it all for me. Last year, after reading the books of Leviticus and Deuteronomy, the Holy Spirit convicted and convinced me to quit, and I did. Let me tell you, Bishop, that "Jesus is the only way" (John 14:6) and we don't need anything else to add to that name.

The Bible says: "And no marvel; for Satan himself is transformed into an angel of light" (2 Corinthians 11:14), whereas Jesus said: "…I am the light of the world…" (John 8:12).

Masons over the years have been reluctant to answer this question: - Why secret codes? Is it biblical, for some to know and others (not members) to remain ignorant? Use your biblical background to seek through it. I have a list of questions for you, which I hope will help you to consider your position as a man of God.

- Are the Masonic rituals (signs, secret codes) biblical? Were they inspired by God through the Holy Spirit like the Bible? Let's think about it...

- Should Christians be in a place with others practicing false religions under the umbrella of God, where the name of Christ is not the center?

- If Christ is the center, why keep Freemasonry a secret from those who are not members? Didn't he die for us all?

- Should Christians gather in a temple where the Koran is accepted?

- How can believers in Christ gather in the same temple with cigarette smokers and drinkers under the umbrella of a god who is being perceived differently among the members?

- What about Masonic penalties to some parts of the body)? Does this sound biblical?

- Do Masons recognize Jesus as the son of God and therefore pray in his name?

- Why not teach the Bible in Masonic temples instead of putting the square and compass on it?

- Can we go to the Father without Christ? John 14:6 has the answer. Why do Masons pray not in the name of Jesus Christ? Not everything with the name of God is godly. The devil calls himself god too, but salvation is only given through **Jesus and Jesus alone.**

- *How can Christians gather in a temple with Muslims who believe in another god and do not recognize Jesus as the son of God?*

- *Doesn't the Bible give only "one name under heaven whereby we must be saved?"(Acts 4:12). Why have secret words? The Bible made it clear not to follow traditions of this world (Romans 12:1) but to be different and to separate ourselves (sanctification). I* **think this is the time for all the schemes that the devil is using to deceive mankind to be exposed in broad day light and for the body of Christ to stand on Jesus alone.** *The world is supposed to be influenced by us, not the other way around.*

God reveals himself only three ways: as the Father, the Son and the Holy Spirit. There are no shortcuts to salvation, it comes only through Jesus. (Acts 4:12).

Since the Lord delivered me from Masonry last year, he gave me an assignment to tell Masons, especially those who are church members and deceived, to get out. I met people who prophesied on me, by letting me know that "the Lord will use you mightily to open up the eyes of deceived men (**to God be the glory!**). He did not let you become a Mason for no reason. He will use you." I've been doing it since then and I will not back down because he is on my side. Amazingly, he puts Masons and cars with Masonic signs on my path almost every day, so I can minister to them. It is amazing about the many testimonies I have since that ministry started. I hope that the Lord will touch your heart, for **he is calling on you to make a U-turn** just like he asked me to do repeatedly in the past.

I thank you for taking the time to read this letter and hope that the Lord will do the rest.

Sincerely yours,

Jean Medois

Jesus is the only way!

Jesus is the answer!

Only Jesus!

Due to the fact that this bishop had given me his business card, when I first met him, I did not have to ask anyone for his information because it was provided to me already. We had no idea then that God was putting something together. Yes, God sees the end from the beginning!

I mailed the letter to him, but weeks and months passed by with no reply. The Lord instructed me to send it again, by only changing the date, but again there was no answer back from him.

In July 2011, I went to the library. One of the employees asked if a particular flash drive left in a computer belonged to anyone there. Its owner had driven away. After a few minutes, a man came back to the library to reclaim the flash drive. Guess what? It was the bishop! The Holy Spirit instructed me to take him to the side and minister to him.

I went straight to him while reminding him of our encounter the previous year. I told him, "Bishop, I am the one that sent you the two letters about Freemasonry, but you have never replied to me." I ministered to him powerfully while he kept his head down. He told me, "God delivered you from Freemasonry because it was not for you." He told me that the Masonic lodge gives him the ability to raise money for the children in the community. He was determined to remain a Mason as he rebuked my call for him to leave the cult. He could not prove to me biblically, why a Christian can be a Mason.

The Lord had me again minister to him with another letter, which you will see as the last chapter of this book. Again, there was no reply. In fact, he had no way of answering those questions even with or without the Bible. I still trust God to deliver him, God was very patient with me and his call for me to leave Freemasonry was persistent. Please keep the bishop in your prayers!

For many deceivers are entered into the world, who confess not that Jesus Christ is come in the flesh. This is a deceiver and an antichrist.

2 John 1:7

Chapter 6

Freemasonry as God Revealed It to Me

What is Freemasonry? According to the Masonic manuals, it is a system of morality veiled in signs and allegory. In this chapter, we are going to analyze certain aspects of It In the light of the Holy Bible.

Is Freemasonry a religion? Is it a deception? Should or can a Christian be a Mason? Let's go to the very first step of any individual as a Mason: the initiation ceremony.

Any man willing to become a member must first go through the initiation process. The very first degree is called: Entered Apprentice. Prior to the ceremony, the individual is divested of his apparel (suit, shirt, tie, jewelry etc.), and provided with a pair of drawers. A slipper in his right foot and left foot is bare. A rope called a Cable tow is placed around his neck and left arm. This is to illustrate that the individual is deprived and in dire need of what they call: The light of Freemasonry (Bible or not?). I must say that all Masons see the rest of the world as being in darkness without the enlightment of Freemasonry. Then, the individual, semi naked, and blindfolded (in darkness), is brought out and, inside the Masonic temple, escorted by the Master of Ceremony and Junior Deacon of the lodge. Now, imagine yourself in that position, not being able to see the number of men assembled in the lodge. Bare breasted, you can only rely on the direction given to you by the person that holds your right arm at the elbow level. Then, you start hearing about penalties, torments, and so on.

Now, remember the individual is blindfolded. So, the sense of sight has been eliminated because they want you to hear carefully without distraction. It would have been different if you were able to see. But you are in darkness and you want to receive the light of Freemasonry. How many lights are there? If you are a Christian already who took part in that ceremony, here is what your Bible says: *"Then spake Jesus again unto them, saying, I am the light of the world: he that followeth me shall not walk in darkness, but shall have the light of life."* (John 8:12). This is what you are supposed to believe, since you call yourself a Christian. Was Christ lying? Because now, you knelt down before a man called the Worshipful Master to receive the light of Freemasonry. Now, since Jesus is the true light of the world and Freemasonry offers light to the new member, do you think the individual will be led to Jesus Christ (Yeshua Hamashiach) at the initiation? Let's find out as the ceremony unfolds...

Once, the initiate enters the lodge, a procession takes place and goes around the temple from west, north, EAST, and south three times. After that, the initiate is invited to kneel down before the altar right at the center of the lodge, with the lights turned off, and the candidate is ready to pronounce the oath of that particular degree. He has no clue about what he is required to repeat after the Worshipful Master of the lodge.

Then, he takes, the Masonic oath. I provide an extract here from each of the first three degrees, the first is, Entered Apprentice: *"All this I solemnly and sincerely swear, with a full and hearty resolution to perform the same, without any evasion, equivocation, or mental reservation, under no less penalty than to have my throat cut across from ear to ear, my tongue plucked out by the roots, and buried in the rough sands of the sea, a cable's length from shore, where the tide ebbs and flows twice in twenty-four hours. So help me God, and keep me steadfast in this obligation of an Entered Apprentice."*

Now, for the Second Degree, which is called Fellow Craft Degree, the oath is as follows: *"All this I solemnly and sincerely swear, with a full and hearty resolution to perform the same, without any evasion, equivocation, or mental reservation, under no less penalty than to have my heart taken from under my naked left breast, and carried to the valley of Jehoshaphat, there to be thrown into the fields to become a prey to the wolves of the desert, and the vultures of the air. So help me, God."*

Finally, for the Third Degree, the last part of the Master Mason's oath or obligation: *"All this I most solemnly and sincerely promise and swear with a full and hearty resolution to perform the same, without any evasion,* equivocation, or mental reservation, under no less penalty than to have my body cut across, my bowels taken out and burnt to ashes, and those ashes scattered to the four winds of heaven; to have my body dissected into four equal parts, and those parts hung on the cardinal points of the compass, there to hang and remain as a terror to all those who shall presume to violate the sacred obligation of a Master Mason."

One may say, "Well, these words are not to be taken literally; they are symbolic and their meanings must be considered as such." Are those oaths or obligations taken out of the Bible? When did God ask men or a certain group to pronounce such? Instead, the Bible says "But above all things, my brethren, swear not, neither by heaven, neither by any other oath: but let your yea be yea; and your nay, nay; lest ye fall into condemnation." (James 5:12).

Here is the first question that should come out of the mouth of a true Christian: Where can I find that in the scriptures, the Holy Bible? Note on that, the candidate is on his knees before a man whom he refers to as the Worshipful Master. I've read the Bible from cover to cover and I have never found that title. Is he a representation of God?

According to the Masonic ritual, these words are being told to the candidate: "Behold your Worshipful Master…" before he shows and tell the initiate about the Masonic due guard, grip, and secret password for that particular degree.

Wait a minute! I am a Christian; I believe in Jesus Christ as my Savior, and his name hasn't been mentioned or introduced to me even once at the initiation. I thought I'd be given my life to Jesus, the true light of the world, "the way, the truth and the life: no man cometh unto the Father but by him." (John 14:6). What happened? Well, my brother, you just renounced Jesus Christ while sworn in to the deceiver, the fake light. "And no marvel; for Satan himself is transformed into an angel of light." (2 Corinthians 11:14). Furthermore, Jesus said: "No man can serve two masters: for either he will hold to the one, and despise the other. Ye cannot serve God and mammon." (Matthew 6:24).

Now, the problem is that you pronounced the oath(s) under harsh penalty and you'll be always fearful to reveal anything to anyone.

If you think clearly, you'll notice that you have been deceived. Now, I am asking myself this logical question: why Masons have to pronounce a pagan-type of oath? What is so secretive about God that only a few can know it? Here is what God says: *"The secret things belong unto the Lord our God: <u>but those things which are revealed belong unto us and to our children forever,</u> that we may do all the words of this law."* (Deuteronomy 29:29). Biblically speaking, all that God reveals belong to all, otherwise, it is a lie. God gave mankind the Holy Bible but it is not restricted to anyone or to any group.

That's why it is important for Christians to know their Bible for the devil uses it too.

Here is what God says through his prophet about the desires of satan:

12. *How art thou fallen from heaven, O Lucifer* (light bearer before he was cast down from heaven) *son of the morning! How art thou cut down to the ground, which didst weaken the nations!*

13. *For thou hast said in thine heart, I will ascend into heaven; I will exalt my throne above the stars of God: I will sit also upon the mount of the congregation, in the sides of the north.*

14. *I will ascend above the heights of the clouds; <u>I will be like the Most High</u>.*

15. *Yet thou shalt be brought down to hell, to the sides of the pit.*

Isaiah 14

The most common problem among some Christians is that they do not believe the Bible entirely. <u>The Bible is the final authority, not men's opinions.</u> If there's anything I'd like God to use me for as you are reading this book it is that you truly fall in love with the Bible and make it your best companion. We cannot believe part of it and ignore the other. God is not confused, but instead his word is eternal. Do not fall for people's opinions if they don't line up with the word of God. I have known great and powerful men that used to voice their opinions on the issues of our time, but when I look around they are no more, just like you and I will be fly away one day, but the word of God will abide forever.

There are many gods in this world, *"Thou shalt have no other gods before me"* (Exodus 20:3). This is our first commandment. Why is God saying that? Let's consider Exodus chapter three, when the Lord came to Moses to send him back to Egypt to deliver the children of Israel. He gave Moses a name: "I AM THAT I AM". One of the reasons for that is, God was about to send Moses into a polytheistic land. The Egyptians served many gods back then, so he had to make a distinction between himself and the idol gods. Throughout the scriptures, that same concept of the true God and other gods is repeated. I beg you, please read your Bible and take time to meditate and allow the Holy Spirit to teach you personally.

Don't fall easily, when you hear people mentioning God. Test the spirit, which god are they talking about? Satan is also a god in this world. If Freemasonry is not about God and his Son Jesus Christ whom he sent to redeem mankind, what should we consider then? The Masonic prayers are not prayed in the name of Jesus as commanded in the Bible (Colossians 3:17). The teachings and standings of Freemasonry are not from Jesus. The rituals are not based on him. Jesus is nowhere to be found in that so-called fraternity. As a matter of fact, the other religious views and beliefs will never accept him in the Masonic lodge.

Instead Freemasonry accepts all the gods of this world in the organization. All of the religions of this world with their gods are welcomed. They make you to believe it is the same God, who manifests himself in all those religions. It is an ecumenical type of society that is deceiving many in the world today. What does the Bible say specifically about that? *"And have no fellowship with the unfruitful works of darkness, but rather reprove them."* (Ephesians 5:11). If you are a Christian, just think about this! One day, you pray in the name of Jesus, and another day you pray to a god accepted under the umbrella of all other religions. Is it right to gather in a temple with others that totally reject Jesus Christ or don't believe that he is God or Lord? Is it right to fellowship with others that believe and pray to other gods? Is it right to gather and fellowship with others that bow down to images and statues? You can realize that every time you are in a Masonic temple you deny Christ.

And Jesus answered and said unto them. Take heed that no man deceive you.

Matthew 24:4

Chapter 7

The Religious Components of Freemasonry

God, the creator of all, manifests himself in only three ways: as the Father, the Son, and the Holy Spirit. *"For there are three that bear record In heaven, the Father, the Word, and the Holy Ghost: and these three are one."* (I John 5:7).

O, my God, thank you, Jesus (Yeshua)! I got it now! The equation is not the way I previously thought, which was: I +I + I = 3. Instead it is: I = I = I.

That's why Jesus says, *"I and my Father are one."* (John 10:30) and the apostle Paul confirmed it: *"And without controversy great is the mystery of godliness: God was manifest in the flesh..."* (I Timothy 3:16).

What's the point here? Jesus (Yeshua) is God! Anything outside of him is of Satan. Anything but Jesus is a deception.

All religions are accepted in Freemasonry. As stated earlier, it is an ecumenical belief system under a generic god called the Grand Architect of the Universe. Too often we hear, "We all serve the same God." The question is: Can you prove it through the Bible? God of the Bible never called himself Allah, Buddha, or any other gods in the world today. On the other hand, Allah does not recognize Jesus (Yeshua) as God, nor does he recognizes Buddha or the other gods of this world. I am not sure how someone can prove that. God of the Bible says: *"I am the Lord: that is my name: and my glory will I not give to another, neither my praise to graven images."* (Isaiah 42:8). People's opinions do not matter. I pray that God opens up your eyes through the reading of his word. When Christians gather in a temple with others that accept other gods, here is what the Bible says: *"Ye adulterers and adulteresses know ye not that the friendship of the world is enmity with God? Whosoever therefore will be a friend of the world is the enemy of God."* (James 4:4).

Is Freemasonry a religion?

1- A <u>deity</u> referred to as the <u>Grand Architect of the Universe (GAOTU)</u> is the god accepted by all Masons under the umbrella of all religions.

2- At the initiation ceremony, a Mason is given a <u>white apron</u> that symbolizes <u>purity</u>.

3- The <u>Masonic prayers</u> are prayed to this generic god (GAOTU).

4- The center of the lodge has an <u>altar</u>.

5- The lodge assembles in a <u>temple</u>.

6- The notion of <u>death and resurrection</u> is part of the Masonic rituals for the Third degree of Master Mason.

7- Masons claim to know the true or the secret <u>name of God</u>: <u>Jahbulon</u>, which was lost, according to them, during the construction of God's temple by Solomon. (Bible or not?)

8- During the funeral service of a Mason, the white apron (<u>purity</u>) is placed upon the body. The Masonic funeral rituals performed relate to <u>heaven</u> as <u>the grand or celestial lodge on high</u> and commit the soul of the deceased Mason to that heavenly lodge. So, in fact, Freemasonry has its own <u>salvation</u>, but not through Jesus Christ.

Furthermore, let's consider this: <u>Where in the Bible does it tell a group or a society to use Boaz, Shibboleth, Tubal-cain and so forth in a secretive manner?</u>

Didn't God say this? *"The secret things belong unto the Lord our God: but those things which are revealed belong unto us and to our children forever, that we may do all the words of this law."* (Deuteronomy 29:29).

So, how come the above words and name are used as secrets in that cult, when they are already given to mankind in the Bible? Think about what God says: the things that are revealed belong unto us, not a group or a secret society, because the word is already given or written for all. Does it make biblical sense?

The devil is a master duplicator. He's in the business of taking God's word and packaging it to create his own. If there's one thing I'd like to allow God to do through me in this book, it is to make you to read, study diligently, meditate, and memorize God's word. I want you to fall in love with the Bible so much that when the deceiver comes your way, he'll find enough word in you to rebuke him in the mighty name of Jesus.

The apostle Paul warned the believers of Galatia to hold on to their faith because he was well aware of the counterfeit works of the enemy intended to derail the true believers. Unto them he said:

6. I marvel that ye are so soon removed from him that called you into the grace of Christ unto another gospel:

7. Which is not another; but there be some that trouble you, and would pervert the gospel of Christ.

8. But though we, or an angel from heaven, preach any other gospel unto you than that which we have preached unto you, let him be accursed.

9. As we said before, so say I now again, if any man preach any other gospel unto you than that we have received, let him be accursed.

Galatians 1

Beware lest any man spoil you through philosophy and vain deceit, after the tradition of men, after the rudiments of the world, and not after Christ.

Colossians 2:8

Chapter 8

Freemasonry Mentioned in the Bible

Where and How?

After repeated calls from God through Bishop Roy E. Brown from the pulpit for me to leave Freemasonry, I did not renounce it. God showed up that time by having me to read the Bible from cover to cover in the year of 2010. It was New Year's Eve, less than two months after my car accident, in Brooklyn, New York, at the Pilgrim Assemblies International, when Bishop Brown asked the ushers to distribute a red pamphlet to those who would read the Bible in one year.

I had started that long journey a few years back, but distractions and trials stopped me along the way. That night, I felt a strong determination deep from within to restart the journey and to finish it with God's help. I prayed over my little booklet containing the daily scriptures, and asked God to help me not to stop this time around.

Indeed, the Lord was waiting for me in the reading of his most holy word. I spent the entire first day of the year locked in my apartment in prayer and fasting. I also read the scriptures assigned on that day. The Lord gave me the strength to continue reading the Bible daily, although hell broke loose on me. It was interesting that, without a car at my disposal, I had more time to concentrate on the word. I was not able to move around the way I used to. God kept me focused and I started to hear the Holy Spirit whispering and ministering to me, about meaning and understanding of the word.

Weeks passed by as I continued to read my Bible daily. It was a very pleasant experience. When I reached a certain chapter in the book of Ezekiel, I heard the Lord through his Holy Spirit telling me, "When I will have you to teach on Freemasonry, I want you to use this text." I couldn't go any further that day as the Lord taught me the things to say about that topic through the light and understanding of his word.

Please grab your Bible and turn to the book of Ezekiel, the eighth chapter. In my King James Version, it is entitled: _The prophet's vision of the abominations in Jerusalem._

God took the prophet Ezekiel in the spirit (a vision) between the earth and the heaven (verse 3) to show him the abominations of the house of Judah that provoked his anger. Mankind thinks if they do certain things in the dark or in secret, God will not see. God is omniscient and he has a way of exposing hidden secrets. Throughout the chapter, God showed Ezekiel different types of abominations, the elders were involved in. One by one he revealed them to his prophet, in verses 6, 13, and 15. He repeatedly said: _"and thou shalt see greater abominations."_

Facing the EAST in Freemasonry--what does that means?

Here is the verse that the Lord gave me concerning Freemasonry and one of its most recognizable practices:

"And he brought me into the inner court of the Lord's house and, behold, at the door of the temple of the Lord, between the porch and the altar, were about five and twenty men, with their backs toward the temple of the Lord, and their faces toward the east; and they worshipped the sun toward the east." (Ezekiel 8:16).

In the Masonic temple, right before the Chaplain's prayer, you hear this: "Brethren, face or observe the EAST". Do you know that every Masonic lodge, I had visited; has an image of the sun in the East of the temple? Do you know the Worshipful Master of the lodge sits in the EAST and that all members are required to behold him in the EAST according to the Masonic rituals? Do you know Masons are required to face the EAST during certain times in their ritualistic works? Do you know that Masons are required to face the EAST while reminding themselves and the lodge of the penalties they are under according the degree being performed? Do you know that Masons are required to stop, face, and salute the Worshipful Master in the EAST, before leaving or crossing over from one side to the other?

The ritualistic works of Freemasonry pertain to the EAST (or the observance of the EAST) to face the sun (where it rises), which is the backbone of Freemasonry. The imagery of the sun is right above the Worshipful Master in the EAST.

Let's go further...

The initiation ceremony as well pertains to the EAST as the candidate is brought forth before the lodge from the west to the EAST to behold the Worshipful Master in the EAST. He pronounces the pagan oath, kneeling down while facing the EAST. Many have said that the individual bows before the Worshipful Master. This is true, but in fact he bows down to the image of the sun in the EAST also. This is just to say the light of Freemasonry is the sun, an idol. This is idol worship! That's why Masons pray facing the East where the sun rises.

Sun worship was widespread in the Babylonian empire. According to this text, Israel (God's chosen people) did as Babylon. Judah followed the practices of idolatry of the heathen that were deeply rooted in them and, even in the leadership.

God warned his people from time to time, not to follow the abominations of the pagan nations. Even in captivity, he gave them the same warnings. In this chapter of Ezekiel, we see an ancient way of worship, known as sun worship which was the way of many pagan nations including Egypt, Greece, and Babylon, and is still present in our time. The fact is, the devil found a way through the centuries to maintain it and to deceive mankind with it. Sun worship is present in Freemasonry. The devil makes Freemasonry interesting and prestigious to Masons and even to church members but God says through the prophet: *"My people are destroyed for lack of knowledge..."* (Hosea 4:6).

Freemasonry is a sophisticated instrument set up by the devil to deceive humanity. Masons are being led to worship ancient Egyptian and Babylonian gods that are illustrated in symbols.

Now, speaking to the body of Christ, I warn you about the infiltration, and in some cases, the acceptance, of secret societies including Freemasonry in your midst. Examine yourself and test the spirit as the Bible says, behind that ecumenical belief system.

Jesus saith unto him, I am the way, the truth, and the life: no man cometh unto the Father, but by me.

John 14:6

Chapter 9

My Last Experience as a Mason

If you have relatives or friends who are Masons, even if they belong to a church, please get yourself busy in prayer on their behalf and, continue to love them. What do I mean by that? Remember when Jesus (Yeshua) said to his disciples, *"This kind can come forth by nothing, but by prayer and fasting."* (Mark 9:29). That's my advice to you today. That deception is so deeply rooted in Mason's souls, that when they are initiated, they are transformed into fanatic machines. Even if they feel deep within them that something is wrong there, they cannot get out; something is holding them. A stronghold has been created on them to the point that they keep on living the lies for years.

That was the position I was in a few years ago. I had tough questions for those guys, but could never ask them. Though, I was deceived, and I always felt and witnessed the illogical and unbiblical aspects of it, I decided to remain a member even after the repeated calls from God.

At the end of 2009, a couple of days after a blizzard had hit the northeastern part of the United States; I decided to attend a Third Degree ceremony in a lodge that belongs in the same Masonic district I was in. I thought it would be canceled, for there were piles of snow everywhere and traffic was still difficult. I called that lodge and was told the degree would go on as scheduled. It was a Friday evening, and I decided to support the members of that particular lodge.

On that evening, seven men were scheduled to become Master Masons, the Third Degree in Freemasonry. The highest Masonic authority of the state of New Jersey, the Grand Master, was present and therefore he led the ceremony. It was a special day for that Masonic temple to host the state leader. Nevertheless, the rituals lasted for hours. They are lengthier for that degree, and they had to be repeated over for seven men. Cigarette breaks were given in between to accommodate the smokers.

As I sat down and enjoyed the ceremony, one thing caught my attention; I had never witnessed such a thing in my time as a Mason. Seven men, knelt down, and blindfolded, squeezed around a small altar to take their Masonic pagan oaths. Six of them swore on a Masonic Bible, and the seventh man, a Muslim had the Koran set in front of him. I was stunned; I knew all religions or faiths are welcomed in Freemasonry, but to experience it, was a whole different thing. It is unbiblical: *"Be ye not unequally yoked together with unbelievers: for what fellowship hath righteousness with unrighteousness? And what communion hath light with darkness?* (2 Corinthians 6:14). Furthermore, the same Apostle Paul told the Ephesians, *"And have no fellowship with the unfruitful works of darkness, but rather reprove them."* (Ephesians 5:11). I entered into deep thoughts and I felt, even at my spiritual level back then, that something was really wrong with that.

Nevertheless, the lengthiest degree ceremony I have ever attended as a Mason ended exactly at 12:07 a.m. Indeed, it was the last degree ceremony I attended, as the Lord was moving to deliver me from that deception, that ecumenical society that have led many to believe we serve the same God.

That's what happens when we don't study the word of God. We are led by the traditions of men (Colossians 2:8), <u>by man-made ideas that are contrary to God's word</u>. In fact, if you had asked those six men, "Do you think or recognize Allah is God?" They would have said, "No." If you had asked that Muslim man, "Did Allah send Jesus Christ to redeem mankind through his blood as the only way?" the answer would have been, "No." <u>How can those men serve the same God?</u> *"For <u>God is not the author of confusion</u>, but of peace, as in all churches of the saints."* (1 Corinthians 14:33).

There are many more questions that could arise between those men that swore in on two different books, but I will let you think, meditate, and pray about it.

When Jesus said, *"I am the way, the truth, and the life: no man cometh unto the Father, but by me."* (John 14:6), was he lying? Please know that the devil is a master duplicator. Choose between God and the lies of the devil, which one you want to believe, for *"God is not a man, that he should lie; neither the son of man, that he should repent..."* (Numbers 23:19).

Jesus (Yeshua) Is the Light of the World

Then spake Jesus again unto them, saying, I am the Light of the world: he that followeth me shall not walk in darkness, but shall have the light of life.

John 8:12

The term "Light of Freemasonry" is nowhere to be found in the Bible, but another (fake) light other than Jesus is mentioned: *"And no marvel; for Satan himself is transformed into an angel of light."* (2 Corinthians 11:14).

The devil has no ability to bring you the full truth. If he apparently brings you one, be aware that there are many lies hidden behind it.

Chapter 10

A Letter to All Christian Masons

It is now the time for this issue to be addressed in the body of Christ according to his word.

Testimony of a Former Thirty-Second Degree Mason

Can a Christian Be a Mason?

I greet you, my brother, in the mighty name of our Lord Jesus Christ (Yeshua Hamashiach). The purpose of this letter is to expose a deception that has been in the world for centuries. I want to refer to secret societies and specifically Freemasonry.

I am Brother Jean Medois, a minister of the gospel of Jesus Christ. I am a former Thirty-Second Degree Mason. I was a member of a Blue Lodge and the Scottish Rite. I held the offices of Junior Steward in my first full year and also served as a Marshal in the second one. Later on, I was named to become a Chaplain, but God intervened and delivered me with his mighty hands.

One may wonder, what is Freemasonry?

Freemasonry is simply "sun worship" or idol worship (Ezekiel 8:16). It is a sophisticated tool created by lucifer to deceive mankind. In Masonry, all rituals take place facing or referring to the EAST, where the sun rises. There is also an image of the sun in the EAST in the Masonic lodge where all Masons are required to turn to during the Masonic rituals.

Now, I want to minister to you that profess to be Christians and Masons at the same time.

1- Do you remember, when you were initiated, you entered the Masonic temple semi naked and, blindfolded, with a cable tow around your neck? Did they give you any biblical references to that? If so, where can I find that application in the Bible?

2- Do you remember when you knelt down, still blindfolded before a man (the Worshipful Master), that "No man can serve two masters..." (Matthew 6:24)? You pronounced a _pagan oath_ (nowhere in the Bible), a curse against yourself that involved penalties and retaliations against your flesh and, your tongue..., to be thrown down to the beasts of the fields. Was that godly? Are there any Biblical references to that?

3- Now, regarding the secret words and names they gave you: Was the name of Jesus mentioned? Acts 4:12 says, "Neither is there salvation in any other: for there is _none other name_ given among men whereby we must be saved."

4- Was Jesus introduced to you at your initiation? Jesus said in John 8:12 "I am the light of the world: he that followeth me shall not walk in darkness, but shall have the light of life." You joined Freemasonry because supposedly you were in darkness and in need of Masonic light, right? But now, here is the question: Where can I find the term "Masonic light" in the Bible?

If you can find it, fine; you may remain a Mason. In case you cannot, my brother, I urge you to call on Jesus because he is the true light of the world. I can also tell you about the fake light: "And no marvel; for Satan himself is _transformed_ into an angel of light." (2 Corinthians 11:14). He used to be in heaven so he knows how to imitate the true light which is Jesus Christ.

The name Lucifer means, light holder or bearer but before he was cast down to the earth by God. If he was able to deceive a number of angels in heaven, how much more, can he deceive us?

In Matthew 4, he came to Jesus with scriptures. Though he used them out of context, he knows the word. The lesson is that, we need to know the word of God for ourselves so well and its proper context, so that when the fake light (Satan) shows up, we can recognize it and rebuke him in the name of Jesus.

5-   Do Masons pray in the name of Jesus? Masons pray to a generic god under the umbrella of all religions, a god referred to as the "Grand Architect of the Universe." but the Bible says, "And whatsoever ye do in word or deed, do all in the name of the Lord Jesus, giving thanks to God and the Father by him." (Colossians 3:17).

6-   If Masonry is of God, why do Masonic temples have bars, where the members can gather and drink all kinds of alcoholic beverages, before or after their meetings?

7-   Where is the notion of secrecy in the Bible? Secret handshakes? Where are the biblical texts for those things? The Bible says: "The secret things belong unto the Lord our God: but those things which are revealed belong unto us and our children forever, that we may do all the words of this law." (Deuteronomy 29:29). Did the Apostle Paul, Moses, John and the others keep God's revelations only to themselves? Therefore, Freemasonry is not of God. It is a satanic cult in which most members do not know what they are involved in. It is a "monkey see, monkey do" type of society.

8-   Just think about it! If Freemasonry or any secret society were that godly or good, don't you think their meetings would be open for all to attend freely? How can the light of Freemasonry be hidden? I thought light was made to be displayed and shine in the darkness, but it seems to me that the light of Freemasonry is not for the entire world; but for a few. I am glad that the true and living God sent his Son Jesus Christ for the whole wide world. "For God so loved the world that he gave his only begotten Son, that whosoever believeth in him should not perish, but have everlasting life." (John 3:16).

I know that Masons do good deeds in their communities for the elderly, in food banks, in blood drives, sponsoring scholarships and so forth but that is the deceptive part of it. The devil uses those good deeds to deceive you so you will remain a member. The devil is in the details: <u>the pagan Masonic rituals that are not from the Bible.</u> The bible says, "Not of works, lest any man should boast." (Ephesians 2:9) and "Knowing that a man is not justified by the works of the law, but by the faith of Jesus Christ, even we have believed in Jesus Christ, that we might be justified by the faith of Christ, and not by the works of the law: for by the works of the law shall no flesh be justified." (Galatians 2:16). Nothing is wrong with giving and helping others, but good deeds won't save you. The Masonic rituals at your funeral won't save you, either. "Jesus saith unto him, I am the way, the truth, and the life: no man cometh unto the Father but by me." (John 14:6).

I know that in the Masonic funeral service, heaven is mentioned as "the celestial lodge on high," which is nowhere to be found in the Bible.

Do you want to be saved? Do this: "That if thou shalt confess with thy mouth the Lord Jesus, and shalt believe in thine heart that God hath raised him from the dead, thou shalt be saved." (Romans 10:9).

<u>Now, keep walking with Jesus because he is THE ONLY WAY.</u>

Jesus is coming back soon for his church, but not for Freemasonry or secret societies because he did not establish them. Instead, here is what he commanded us to do: "And he said unto them, Go ye into all the world, and preach the gospel to every creature." (Mark 16:15). <u>Is there anything secretive about the gospel he asked us to preach? Why would Jesus say that, if we all serve the same God?</u>

May the Lord bless you and keep you and may his face shine upon you. May he reveal even more to you (Jeremiah 33:3) in the name of Jesus (Yeshua).

Brother Jean Medois

First posted on Facebook in summer 2012

This letter has been modified from the original text for the purpose of this book

A Prayer for the Body of Christ Worldwide

Dear Heavenly Father, in the mighty name of Jesus Christ (Yeshua Hamashiach), I thank and praise you as I come before your throne of grace for your people, O Lord, the body of Christ. We are all sinners, and I ask you, Lord, to blot out all of our sins, iniquities and transgressions.

Lord, because of our disobedience to your word, we have fallen and gone astray from your presence. Consequently, the body of Christ has been penetrated by false teachings, doctrines, and even by secret societies, O Lord!

Many, O Lord, are perishing from lack of knowledge. Many under-shepherds are in darkness, and are members of secret societies while leading your people. They do not know the true light themselves, Lord; how can they continue to lead your people to Jesus Christ, the true light of the world? How long, O Lord, will you allow this to happen? How long will you allow the world to penetrate the church? The principles of the world are being taught inside your house, where true doctrines and biblical principles are nowhere to be found. O Lord, your people are being hijacked by false teachers and preachers.

Arise, O Lord and save your people! We need your presence and the leading by your Holy Spirit back to your house. Destroy all worldly influences and idols in the body of Christ. Send true teachers and pastors to lead your people. Set the church free of Freemasonry and other secret societies.

The time has come, Lord, for your people to wake up from their spiritual sleep and to be set free from all worldly influences. The time has come for the gospel to be preached to all nations. I pray, O Lord, for a harvest of souls in all continents. May your power come down and overtake this wicked and sinful world.

Bring your people back to prayer and fasting, O Lord. Bring your people back to Bible study and give us the desire to study your word for ourselves, for it contains all truths.

O Lord, the world is dying because we don't know who we are; I pray that you reveal yourself to us. I pray that you save those in the churches who are Masons, or who are involved in any secret societies.

May your name be magnified, glorified, and be lifted up above all, for the earth is the Lord's, and the fullness thereof and they that dwell therein. In the name of Jesus (Yeshua) I pray, amen.

Neither is there salvation in any other: for there is none other name under heaven given among men, whereby we must be saved.

Acts 4:12

His name is Jesus (Yeshua)

And be not conformed to this world: but be ye transformed by the renewing of your mind, that ye may prove what is that good, and acceptable, and perfect, will of God.

Romans 12:2

To God be the glory!

Made in the USA
Charleston, SC
28 October 2013